COURSE OF AMMUNITION FOR BOYS.

By Authority of the Lords Commissioners of the Admiralty.

CORRECTED TO JANUARY 1915.

ADMIRALTY,
   GUNNERY BRANCH,
      G. 6557/14.

The Naval & Military Press Ltd

Published by

The Naval & Military Press Ltd
Unit 5 Riverside, Brambleside
Bellbrook Industrial Estate
Uckfield, East Sussex
TN22 1QQ England

Tel: +44 (0)1825 749494

www.naval-military-press.com
www.nmarchive.com

In reprinting in facsimile from the original, any imperfections are inevitably reproduced and the quality may fall short of modern type and cartographic standards.

BOYS' COURSE OF AMMUNITION.

THE aim of this course is to teach boys and youths to know the various classes of Ammunition, and stores connected therewith, by sight, their use, and where they are to be found in a seagoing ship. Useful information concerning Magazines and Shell Rooms, Prepare for War, Clear for Action, General Quarters, and Night Defence is included, in order to explain the meaning of these terms.

Guns.

The principal guns used in the **Naval Service** are:—

15-inch, 13·5-inch and 12-inch.—Mounted in battleships and battle cruisers.

9·2-inch.—Mounted in cruisers.

7·5-inch.—Mounted in cruisers.

6-inch.—Mounted in cruisers, light cruisers; also form the secondary armament and anti-torpedo boat armament of some battleships.

4·7-inch.—Mounted in light cruisers and gunboats.

4-inch.—Mounted in light cruisers, gunboats, and destroyers as main armament, also in battleships and battle cruisers for defence against torpedo craft.

3-inch Q.F.—Semi-automatic on anti-aircraft mountings with maximum elevation 90°—mounted in the latest battleships.

12-pr.—Mounted in earlier battleships and cruisers for defence against torpedo craft, also in light cruisers, gunboats and destroyers.

3 and 6-pr.—Mounted in older destroyers, torpedo boats, and cruisers. Also used for screwing into breech of larger guns for practice when they are called "Sub-Calibre Guns."

Maxims.—For boat and shore service.

NOTE 1.—Guns are measured by the diameter of the bore. Light guns by the weight of the projectile thrown.

NOTE 2.—A Q.F. gun is distinguished from a B.L. gun in having the charge made up in a brass cylinder instead of a silk cloth bag ; this obviates the necessity for obturation and sponging.

Explosives.

An explosive is a substance which on being ignited is rapidly converted into a volume of gas. This gas if confined, as in the chamber of a gun, sets up pressure and so propels the projectile through the gun into the air.

The two explosives, used in the Service, for guns, are Gunpowder and Cordite.

Gunpowder.

This explosive is now used for Blank charges, bursting shell, igniting Cordite charges, and also in fuzes and tubes.

Gunpowder is a mixture of Charcoal, Saltpetre, and Sulphur in certain definite proportions.

It is manufactured in various sizes from half-inch cubes down to practically dust.

The larger sizes are used for the bursters of large shell, and Blank charges, and the smaller sizes for igniters of Cordite charges, and in fuzes and tubes.

Cordite.

This is a smokeless explosive, and is used as a propellant for all guns.

Cordite is a mixture of Nitro-glycerine, Gun-cotton and vaseline.

It is used in the form of brown sticks of various sizes; each size is known by a number which is roughly the number of 100ths of an inch in its diameter; for instance, size 50 would be $\frac{50}{100}$ of an inch, or $\frac{1}{2}$ an inch in diameter, and so on. Generally speaking, the largest Cordite is used for the largest guns.

Cordite is a much more powerful explosive than powder, but burns slower and is harder to ignite; for this reason powder igniters are attached to all Cordite charges.

Lyddite.

This is a very powerful explosive made of Picric acid, and is used for bursters for Lyddite shell. The Lyddite is poured into the shell in a molten condition and solidifies on cooling.

High Explosives.

Two other high explosives are used for bursters for shell and are termed Composition Exploding and Trotyl.

Cartridges.

The charges for guns are made up in Cartridges for convenience, safety, and rapidity in loading. B.L. cartridges are put in a bag made of silk cloth, as this is strong and does not smoulder in the gun so much as other materials.

Cordite charges are made of Cordite sticks, tied up in a bundle with silk twist, and then placed in a bag; at one end of this bag is sewn a shalloon bottom containing R.F.G.[2] powder, to form an igniter, this ignites easily and lights the Cordite.

The igniters on 7·5″ and above cartridges are protected by a disc of cardboard covered with silk cloth marked with a red cross and fitted with a becket marked "Tear off."

All the discs must be torn off in handing room when loaded by power and at the gun when loaded by hand.

All B.L. cartridges are marked in ink with their weight, the gun they are to be fired in, and other information.

Drill cartridges are supplied to ships of the same shape, size, and weight as the proper charges. For B.L. guns they are covered with raw hide or canvas.

Charges are known as "Full," "Practice," or "Blank" according to the amount used; the "Practice" charge being $\frac{3}{4}$ except in the case of the 6″ B.L., which is either $\frac{1}{2}$ or $\frac{3}{4}$ according to the method of making up, and the 4″ B.L. which is always a full charge.

Blank charges are supplied to saluting ships for the saluting guns, to non-saluting ships for the heaviest gun allowed blank.

Q.F. cartridges consist of an inner bundle of cordite sticks, secured by silk or shalloon braid, outside which is placed the remainder of the cordite sticks, the lower ends of these are tied with silk into small bundles so as to form an enlarged base to the charge.

In the centre of the rear end is placed a Cordite cylinder containing a little bag of powder to act as an igniter. The charge is then placed in a brass case, with the Cordite cylinder surrounding the igniter in the centre of the base of the cartridge. The front end is closed by a white metal lid, carefully fastened in place. Metal igniters are superseding the cordite cylinders and igniters.

3-inch Q.F., 6 and 3-pr. ammunition is called fixed ammunition and has the shell secured to the cartridge, like a rifle cartridge.

Blank charges are in similar cases to Service ammunition (with the 6 and 3 pr. the cases are shorter), and when filled a metal lid is not used, except for 6" and 4·7" Q.F., but a felt wad is employed instead. Blank charges for guns are always of powder.

Dummy and drill cartridges are supplied for Q.F. guns. Dummy cartridges are painted black, and, being only supplied for exercising ammunition parties, are not to be placed in the gun.

Tubes.

All guns above 6-prs. are fired by means of tubes, except those fired by percussion primers. Vent sealing brass tubes are used for B.L. and Q.F. guns fired by percussion or electricity. B.L. and Q.F. guns are usually fired by electricity, using an electric tube.

The two P. tubes (P. electric wireless and percussion) must be known; these can be told apart by their heads and colour, the P. electric wireless has a tin disc sunk in a black insulating material in the centre of the head, and is a plain brass tube. The P. percussion is easily distinguished by being black, and having four notches in the head.

These tubes are supplied in flat tin boxes made watertight, red lettering for Percussion Tubes, black for Electric Tubes. The latest pattern Electric Tube is the Mark VII. electric, the latest Percussion Tube is the V.S. Percussion Mark VII.

All the latest B.L. guns, 4" to 15", have a larger vent and use "large" electric and percussion tubes. These are similar to the earlier or "small" tubes, but larger; the latest mark of P. electric "large" is the Mark IV., and the latest P. percussion "large" is the Mark II. In addition to the above a new tube, the "S." electric, has now been introduced for use in guns which are fitted

A 4

with strikerless locks. These tubes are similar to the P. electric large, but have a raised contact piece in the head.

Percussion drill tubes (large and small) are milled around the head, which has a piece of indiarubber in the centre, also there are four long grooves in the body. Fired electric tubes are used for drill in electric firing, both at the gun and loading teacher.

Short quill friction tubes are still used in the Service for firing the 1-lb. Signal Rockets. These are being replaced by copper friction tubes.

Bronze adaptors are supplied in Q.F. cartridges, and electric or percussion tubes are fired in them.

Percussion primers are supplied in the cartridges for the 4" Marks IV. and V., 3" Mark I., and 12-pr. 4-cwt. Q.F. guns. They screw in flush with the base, and are protected by a clip similar to that used with the 6 and 3 prs.

Tubes are stowed in the Gunner's storerooms in a special tin-lined locker. For ready use steel boxes are now fitted for the stowage of tubes as follows:—One box to every turret, 7·5" and above; one box to every two or less guns using "large tubes," one box to every three or less guns using "small tubes."

Hand extractors are used at B.L. guns when the tube jambs in the vent. The breech carrier arm and boxslide are cut away to admit of their use.

The following instruments are used for keeping the tube chambers and vent clear of fouling during firing:—Rimer for clearing the tube chamber; vent bit for clearing the vent beyond the tube chamber. A new instrument has now been introduced combining the duties of the rimer and vent bit, and is known as a vent clearer. Other vent instruments are the tube chamber borer for clearing a broken tube from the tube chamber, and a drift, for forcing back a jambed tube.

Vent implements will be found at the gun. For Q.F. guns we have separate keys for inserting and removing adaptors, the long one being used for removing them after firing; a cartridge holder resembling tongs is then used to hold the cartridge.

These implements are to be found on the gun deck in a box.

Powder Cases, Boxes, &c.

Charges are supplied to ships packed in boxes, which are either made of metal or of wood with a metal lining, so that they can be made air and water tight for the preservation of the contents.

The cases most generally met with are :—

- (a) Cylindrical cases; they are used for stowing charges for turret guns.
- (b) The rectangular corrugated, made of brass, and used for hand-loaded B.L. guns ; these cases have a small round lid in one end, and are opened with a metal key.
- (c) Outfit boxes, made of wood lined with zinc; they are used for charges for quick-firing guns above 6-pr. To open them the lid can be unlocked with a Mark IV. metal key and can then be pulled off.
- (d) Metal-lined cases are made of wood lined with metal, and are used for various small cartridges, especially rifle ammunition for boat work. They are opened by unscrewing two screws in the lid, using a "metal-lined key"; the lid is then opened and the metal bung pulled off. This bung is covered with luting round the edge, so that when replaced it makes the case watertight again, and it is for this reason that the case is used in boats.
- (e) The Small Arm Ammunition box and half-box, made with wood lined with tin. They are used for rifle, pistol, and aiming rifle ammunition; pistol is always in half-boxes, aiming rifle in whole boxes.

  NOTE.—(a) and (b) are now made so that when stowed in the magazine the lids can be weakened. This is done to prevent serious damage by explosion in the event of a charge deteriorating; the weakened lids would be blown off before the gas reaches a high pressure.

To open these cases no key is required, a pin securing the lid must be pulled out, and the lid, which is wedge-shaped, can then be knocked out; the tin lid below, which is soldered on, can be pulled off.

6 and 3 pr. have special boxes; 6-pr. being in oblong stone-coloured boxes, 11 in a box; 3-pr. is in square grey-coloured boxes, 16 in a box. The cartridges go in base up with a clip over the base to protect the cap. To open these boxes, uncatch and open the lid, then pull out the square metal lid inside.

Boxes containing Practice ammunition have the lid painted yellow and stencilling in black. Boxes containing lyddite are painted yellow all over.

All boxes (except Small Arm boxes) containing Service ammunition will be marked with two red bands.

All boxes containing Small Arm ammunition have special coloured marks to show the contents. Those in general use now are for ·303″ ball Cordite, pistol Cordite, and 1″ Aiming Rifle ammunition. These must be known. All Cordite ammunition has a red mark, except ·303″ Cordite for short range practice, which is yellow, and ·303 Mark VII., which is green.

Small Arm ammunition is packed in paper packets, for rifle containing 10, for pistol 6.

Boxes containing Blank ammunition (except in case of rifle and machine gun) are painted red.

Boxes containing Dummy ammunition are painted black. For passing B.L. cartridges from the magazines to the guns there are special cases intended to protect the charge on the way, and to be convenient to carry; these are called waterproof duck cases, and they are supplied to all B.L. guns, each holding a full, half, or quarter charge according to nature of gun. They are stored in handing room. To Destroyers armed with the 4″ B.L. Mark VIII. gun, Clarkson's cases are supplied, holding six cartridges.

For transporting ammunition for Q.F. guns above 6-pr., bags are supplied holding 1, 2, or 4 shells or cartridges, those for cartridges being red, those for projectiles being white.

To face page 10. *Plate I.*

DISTINGUISHING MARKS FOR S.A. AND M.G. AMMUNITION BOXES.

Devices of the colours & forms shown are used to distinguish packages & boxes of the several descriptions of small arm & machine gun ammunition mentioned

 1 INCH ELECTRIC AIMING RIFLE

 WEBLEY SCOTT SELF-LOADING ·455

 ·45 MACHINE GUN BALL CARTRIDGE

 M^K VII ·303 INCH
If in "Chargers" the word "Chargers" is printed diagonally across, if in bandoliers, as on label.

 ·303 RIFLE BALL IN PACKETS

 ·22 AIMING RIFLE

 MORRIS AIMING TUBE ·23

 CARTRIDGE S.A. DUMMY DRILL MAGAZINE RIFLE

 CARTRIDGE S.A. ·303 CORDITE SHORT RANGE PRACTICE

 PISTOL WEBLEY ·441″

 S.A. BALL ·303″ IN CHARGERS

The various stores mentioned are to be found in a ship as follows :—Keys for opening cases are hung up in the magazines where they are wanted. Bags are kept in the magazines and shell rooms, about two-thirds in the magazines.

Projectiles.

The following marks on a projectile will indicate its nature and in conjunction with Plates II. and III., the various types will be easily distinguished. *All* projectiles are painted black, *except* High Explosive, which are yellow, and 12-pr., 12 and 8 cwt., grey, to distinguish them from other 12-pr. projectiles :—

A white tip denotes a shot (now only used for practice).

A red tip denotes shrapnel shell.

A white band denotes a Common shell; two white bands denote an Armour-piercing shell.

A red band on shoulder denotes projectile is filled.

A red band on the body of a high explosive shell denotes that it contains " Composition Exploding," a green band that it contains " Trotyl," and a black band that it is supplied for drill only. Shells filled with lyddite are painted yellow, no band on body.

A yellow band half-way down denotes practice projectile.

Black band on lyddite denotes dummy projectile.

The following are the projectiles supplied to the Navy and their use :—

A.P. Shell are supplied to all guns 6-inch and above for attacking heavy armour. They are fitted with a mild steel cap.

Common Shell.—Supplied to all guns to attack unarmoured or lightly armoured parts of a ship. They are made thinner in the walls than A.P. so as to contain a larger burster, and therefore are not strong enough to get through heavy armour. Common shell are fitted with caps for the latest guns, 6-inch and above.

Shrapnel Shell.—Supplied to all guns 12-pr. and above for use against exposed bodies of men. They contain large numbers of lead balls; the size and number vary with calibre of gun. On exploding, these balls scatter over a large area.

High Explosive.— Supplied to all guns, and are intended for use instead of common shell as they have a much more destructive effect.

All shell have the calibre of gun and mark of projectile stencilled on the head in white paint (except high explosive, which have it in black).

Various stores found or used with projectiles are as follows :—

Fuze Protectors are used to protect early pattern base fuzes during transport.

Grommets are found on projectiles when drawn to protect the driving band, but must be removed before the projectile is entered into the gun.

Lifting bolts are used for lifting certain earlier pattern heavy projectiles; they screw into a hole in the side, a plug being first unscrewed.

Lifting bands are provided for convenience in transporting shell.

A grab is supplied to 7·5-inch mountings and above for lifting projectiles.

Gauges are used for gauging all projectiles before firing, and are stowed in the shell room.

All common and A.P. shell are filled as full as possible with pebble and grain powder or high explosive.

The bursting charge is always put in a bag or container.

All necessary information concerning a projectile is to be found on its cap, body and base.

The copper band on the lower part of a projectile is called the "driving band." On the projectile being forced through the bore the copper bites into grooves of the rifling, and so gives the projectile its spin which keeps it point on during its flight; it also prevents any escape of gas past the projectile.

There are numerous types and designs of driving bands, which vary with the calibre and type of projectile.

Some driving bands are made of copper and nickel, and are known as the Cupro Nickel driving band. When a projectile is fitted with this band, it is distinguished by having a white band painted immediately above the driving band.

Tracers.—To enable the flight of a projectile to be traced, Night and Day Tracers have been introduced. Of the former, there are internal for separate ammunition and external for fixed ammunition. The internal tracers screw into the projectile flush with the base, and the external tracers screw into a socket protruding from the base. Day tracers consist of a cavity in the shell filled with a black liquid. A very small hole permits of this liquid escaping during the flight of the shell, thus leaving a small black trail in the air. Night Tracers contain a burning composition which is ignited when the projectile leaves the muzzle of the gun, and leaves a small trail of fire in the air. With Day Tracers and external Night Tracers no steps need be taken on board ship, but internal tracers have to be inserted in lyddite shell or practice shot before firing. Internal Tracers are stowed in the Gunner's Storeroom, 10 in a sealed cylinder. The marks on projectiles referring to Tracers are as follows :—

Night Tracers.—

When fitted with Night Tracer.

When fitted for, but not with Night Tracer. (A plug would be in base of shell.)

Day Tracers.—

When fitted with Day Tracer (*i.e.*, the cavity is filled with liquid).

When fitted for, but not with, Day Tracer. (In this case there would be no liquid in the cavity provided for it.)

These symbols would be stencilled in black on yellow shells, and in red on black shells.

Fuzes.

Fuzes are used to burst shell.

There are three kinds of fuzes in the Service :—
  (1) Percussion Fuzes, which burst the shell on grazing or striking anything.
  (2) Time fuzes, which burst the shell at any given range.
  (3) Time and Percussion, which burst the shell at any given range during flight or on striking anything.

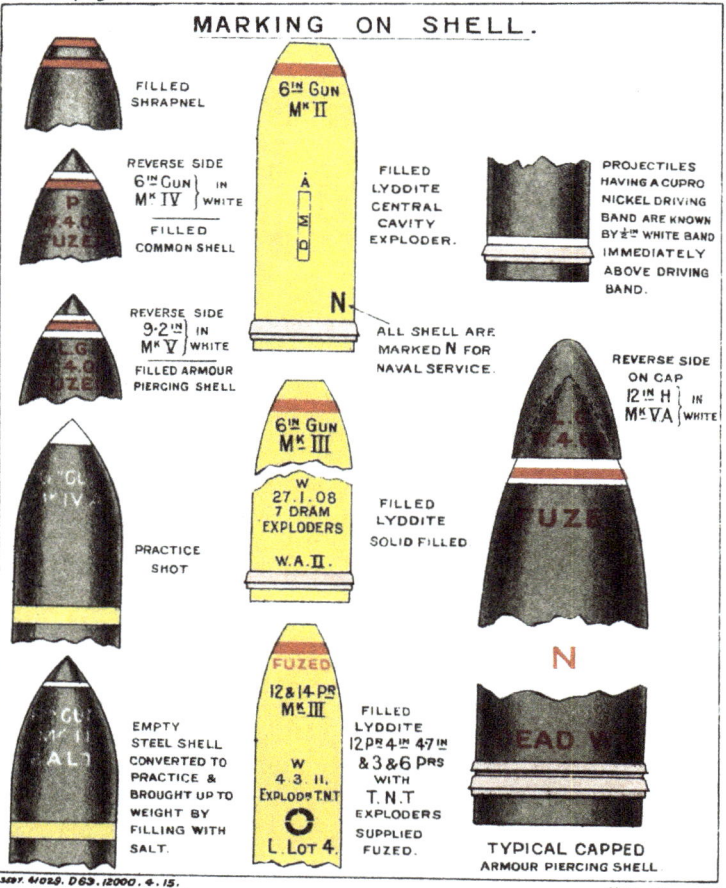

The Various Fuzes in General Use are :—

Percussion and Direct Action Impact for lyddite.

Base Percussion, large, for A.P. and common shell, 6-inch and above.

Base Percussion, medium, for common 12-pr. to 4·7.

Hotchkiss Base Percussion, for 3 and 6-pr. and 3-pr. Vickers.

Time and Time and Percussion, for shrapnel shell.

To burst a Shrapnel Shell with a Time or Time and Percussion Fuze during flight :—

We know from actual experiment the length of time any given projectile takes to travel any distance, also the length of time a train of powder takes to burn, therefore we can tabulate a scale (called a fuze scale) comparing range with a length of powder train inside the fuze. This train is divided into divisions ; as an example, 3,000 yards equals $12/\frac{3}{4}$ divisions for a 12-pr. gun, which means that by the time the projectile has reached 3,000 yards the powder will be burnt to the $12/\frac{3}{4}$ division. By revolving the composition ring which contains the powder train to the $12/\frac{3}{4}$ division we can arrange for the fuze to go off and so burst the shell.

This fuze can be used as a time or percussion fuze, or both, but if using it as a time fuze care must be taken to take out the percussion pin as well as the time.

Base percussion fuzes must be examined before firing, to see that they are properly screwed in and undamaged. (With 6 and 3 pr. this cannot be done.) Great care must be taken in handling base-fuzed shell.

Fuzes are kept in the shell rooms packed in airtight tin boxes, these are packed in wooden boxes.

Base fuzed shell are supplied fuzed, but a few spare fuzes are supplied to replace any damaged ones.

Nosed fuzed shell must never be unloaded from a gun, but must be fired away.

Direct Action fuzes are fitted with a cap which is kept on until the shell is just being entered in the gun, when projectile loader removes it and reports " Cap off."

Nose fuzes are screwed into the nose of the shell, the plug being first taken out by the Service fuze key.

For Base fuzes a base fuze-and-plug key is used.

Only the proper keys supplied are ever to be used when fuzing or unfuzing shell.

Fuze keys are found at the gun.

Fireworks.

Fireworks are supplied to a ship in a fireworks' box which is stowed in the shell room. The Box is opened with metal lined key.

The fireworks found in a ship are short lights, signal rocket, Very's cartridges; and in addition port-fires and slow match are carried. Short lights burn for one-and-a-half minutes; and are used for signalling and illuminating purposes.

Short lights are supplied fitted with a handle with a plug in the bottom; to light them, the cap is torn off, the plug taken out, and the inner end is drawn across the top of the light, which will catch fire.

Signal Rockets are used for signalling purposes; they are fired on board ship from a rocket tube, by means of 'a short quill friction tube or copper friction tube. On putting the rocket in the tube a stick must be attached; this stick is always found in the tube, and is attached to the rocket by a tongue on the side, the rocket stick having a small piece cut away to take the tongue. Spare sticks are kept close by, generally under the Fore Bridge.

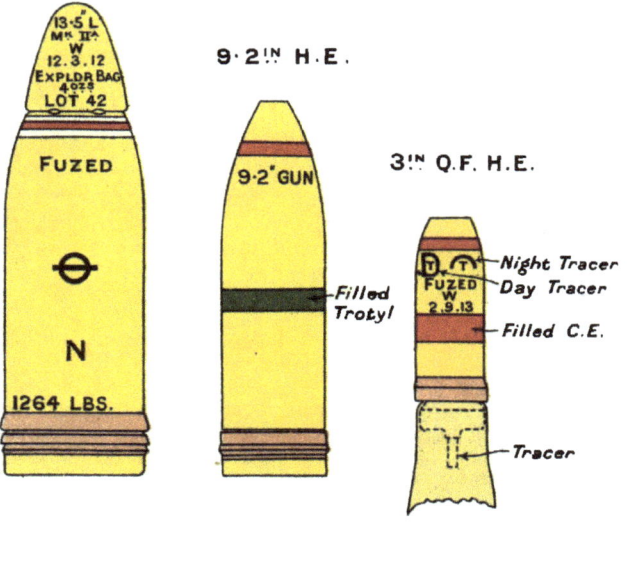

The rocket can be fired without a rocket-tube by using a stick about 18 inches long with a rope tail. The rocket is held in the hand and lit with a port-fire or a piece of slow match secured to anything convenient. When fired in this way the hand must be kept clear of the back fire. This is the way to fire a rocket from a boat.

NOTE.—The 1-lb. Signal Rocket is being superseded by the "Rocket, Flash and Sound," which is really a Signal and Sound Rocket combined.

Sound Rockets are designed to give a loud report in the air; before firing a stick is attached to the rocket, a charge with a detonator is placed in the head, and the plug is replaced on top of the rocket. It is lit by means of a port-fire and fired from a special wooden stand. These rockets are only supplied to ships doing steam trials without any ammunition on board, or ships without guns; for signalling purposes.

Rockets and short or signal lights are supplied in airtight tin boxes holding one.

Very's cartridges are supplied for signalling, they are brass cartridges with a coloured cardboard end showing the colour they burn. Three colours are supplied, Red, White and Green. In the dark the colours can be told by feeling the rim of the base; red is milled (like the edge of a shilling) all round the base, white is milled halfway, and green is smooth.

Very's cartridges are fired with a Very's pistol, Mark II. or III.; to load Mark II., set it at half-cock, open the pistol by pulling out the catch underneath, put in the cartridge, close the pistol, then full-cock it, and fire it in the air, when a star of the colour required is shot out, finally half-cock, open the pistol and throw out the fired case. The Mark III. pistol is loaded in a similar manner to the Webley Pistol.

The pistol is kept with the cartridges.

Port-fires are used for lighting rockets or setting fire to anything, they burn 12 to 15 minutes, and generally cannot be put out by water. They can be lit by anything if dry at the end, and are put out by cutting off the burning end, saving the remainder.

Slow match is hemp soaked in a special liquid; it is generally used for keeping a light going, as in a boat. It burns at the rate of 1 yard in eight hours, and a yard weighs about a quarter of a pound.

Some other fireworks are occasionally supplied to a ship for illuminating. As, however, fireworks may be wanted at any time in a hurry, or in boats, a certain number are kept in boxes for the upper deck and boats.

These boxes are the Night Signal box, Sea Boats' boxes and Boats' magazines.

The Night Signal box contains three signal rockets, one tin of friction tubes, 12 Very's cartridges (four of each colour), two Short Lights Mark II., one Very's pistol, and 60 rounds of rifle blank ammunition. As a rocket is the signal for "Man overboard," the rocket tube is always kept ready loaded at sea.

Whenever fireworks are suddenly wanted on board, the Night Signal box is the proper place to go for them.

A Sea Boat's box is supplied for each sea boat; they contain four short lights, 10 Very's Lights (five red and five green) and pistol.

One of these boxes is placed in each sea boat on the ship going to sea.

Boats' magazines contain two Signal Rockets, two sticks with rope tails, and two Port-fires, also pistol ammunition in a pouch, a metal-lined key, and 1-lb. Slow Match.

A Gig's magazine contains one Signal Rocket, one stick with rope tail, one Port-fire, one metal-lined key, 1-lb. Slow Match, and pistol ammunition in a pouch.

Lifebuoys.

Two sorts of lifebuoys are supplied to ships: one is the ordinary round cork buoy known as Kisbies; the other is the metal buoy hung on the ship's side by a slip worked from inboard, and on which a sentry is placed at sea. This buoy has two Calcium lights, which catch fire on the buoy touching the water, and burn with a bright flame, white smoke, and bad smell; this light or its smoke is intended to show clearly the position of the buoy at any time.

Should they not burn, or in a fog, there is a whistle on the buoy, which can be used to attract attention.

Magazines and Shell Rooms.

Magazines are built as watertight tanks, in older ships these are lined with wood. A bulkhead cuts off part to form a handing room, and it is from the handing room that the charges are sent to the guns.

Magazines are fitted with ventilating inlets and outlets, also cooling facilities and arrangements for flooding the magazine in case of fire, and an air-escape valve.

Before going into one, knife, and generally cap and jumper, must be taken off, and stowed neatly in the proper place, which will be pointed out outside. On going into a magazine the Ventilating inlet and outlet must first be opened by the wheels generally to be found in the handing room. The electric light will be switched on by the G.M., or a Torpedo man.

The ammunition cases are stowed in bays, which are all marked with their proper contents.

All charges are taken out of their boxes and passed to the handing room through scuttles in the doors. Ready racks, or "bottle racks" for Q.F. cartridges are fitted in the magazine near the door.

Shell rooms have no handing rooms.

The shell are stowed in bays all properly marked with the contents, and in some ships, shell for certain guns are stowed in racks in the ammunition passage near the shell hoist.

Magazines and shell rooms are lit by light boxes outside, or by "bunker lights" in recent ships, two sets to each magazine on separate circuits; by candles as an alternative, also by portable hand lamp (electric).

Note on Handling Ammunition.

Whenever ammunition is being moved, as when getting it in or out of the ship, clearing or stowing a magazine or shell room, it must not be thrown about or handled roughly, and must not be landed heavily on the deck or the ammunition will be damaged and found useless, if not dangerous, when wanted.

Hoisting shell with lifting bolt, care should be taken that the bolt is not unscrewed by the projectile turning round while in transit.

Prepare for War.

When war is declared, ships are at once prepared for war by landing gear not required in war time, fuzing Lyddite shell, and filling shot racks with the proper projectiles.

All possible gear aloft or about the decks is lashed, got down or stowed below the armoured deck, and everything is done that the Captain thinks best to add to the fighting power of his ship, and to free his decks of encumbrances.

Clear Ship for Action.

During war time when in the vicinity of the enemy the final preparation for fighting would be made, that is, the ship is cleared for action by putting down the rails on the forecastle and poop, clearing away everything left in the way of working the guns, stowing mess tables out of the way, and generally removing everything left after Prepare for War that would interfere with the fighting of the ship.

Action or General Quarters.

When the ship is cleared for action, "Action," or in peace time if not about to fire, "General Quarters" would be sounded.

At this bugle every man goes to his quarters, guns are cleared away, ammunition is passed up and the guns are loaded ready for the bugle "Commence Firing." If "General Quarters" (Action bugle with one G) is sounded, only Dummy ammunition is passed up for the guns. Magazinemen never open up ammunition unless it is required for firing.

Night Defence.

This station is primarily for repelling attacks by Torpedo Craft at night, but provision is also made in the event of meeting an enemy's big ship at night.

All the small guns are manned with full crews, and the larger guns with reduced crews.

Men are also detailed for searchlights, look-outs, &c.

The guns are divided into groups, and controlled by officers and men in convenient positions above the guns.

The searchlights are controlled separately. Everything is prepared before dark, *i.e.*, ammunition supplied, shelters rigged, communications (flexible voice-pipe) rigged between the officers' positions and the guns.

If an immediate attack is not expected a proportion of the guns' crews remain below turned in, and only some of the guns are manned. If the ship is attacked, fire is at once opened, and the men below come up at once to their stations. The guns are loaded and at half-cock, ready to open fire at once, the Sightsetter wearing the headpiece, so as to be ready to pass orders.

www.ingramcontent.com/pod-product-compliance
Lightning Source LLC
Chambersburg PA
CBHW060227050426
42446CB00013B/3212